Pray the Rosary

A Walk with Jesus and Mary

Maria Grace Dateno, FSP,
and Marianne Lorraine Trouvé, FSP

Boston

Nihil Obstat: Reverend Thomas W. Buckley, S.T.D., S.S.L.

Imprimatur: ✠ Seán Cardinal O'Malley, O.F.M. Cap.
Archbishop of Boston
November 28, 2016

ISBN 10: 0-8198-6041-7 ISBN 13: 978-0-8198-6041-5

Cover design by Rosana Usselmann

Cover art: E. Murillo, Madonna of the Rosary

Published by Pauline Books & Media, 50 Saint Pauls Avenue, Boston, MA 02130-3491. www.pauline.org

Printed in the U.S.A.

Pauline Books & Media is the publishing house of the Daughters of St. Paul, an international congregation of women religious serving the Church with the communications media.

3 4 5 6 7 8 9 10 25 24 23 22 21

Introduction

So, you want to pray the Rosary? You're in good company. The Rosary has been the prayer of saints and sinners for centuries!

The Rosary is a powerful prayer because meditation on the life of Jesus brings us closer to him and helps us to grow in love. Mary is the person who is closest to Jesus, so when we ask her to pray for us, she helps us to grow in love for him.

The Rosary has various elements or components that are adaptable to each person's needs. The combination of vocal prayer (prayers spoken aloud) and mental prayer (reflection or meditation) means one can shift one's focus to whichever aspect is helpful at the moment one is praying.

Meaning of the Words: Some people focus on the meaning of the words in the prayers of the Rosary, including the Our Father, Hail Mary, and Glory, especially when they are still becoming familiar with the prayers. The two prayers that make up most of the Rosary have their basis in Scripture. Matthew 6:9–13 is where we find the Our Father, and Luke 1:28 and 1:42 contain the words of the first half of the Hail Mary. The words themselves are beautiful and can fuel our prayer for a long time.

Meditation on the Mysteries: Often the words of the Our Father and Hail Mary gradually fade into the background and provide a setting or atmosphere for reflection on the mysteries. The mysteries are events in the life of Jesus and Mary, and there are four sets: Joyful, Luminous, Sorrowful, and Glorious. We call them mysteries not because we are trying to solve or figure them out, but because they are mysterious—we can never grasp them completely. While praying each decade (set of 10 Hail Marys) some people try to imagine the scene of that particular mystery, as if they were part of it or watching from nearby. One can also reflect on a word, attitude, or desire of Jesus, Mary, or another character in the mystery. The art for each mystery in this booklet, as well as the quotations from Scripture, can help this meditation.

Fruit of the Mysteries: Another way to pray the Rosary involves focusing on the "fruit" of each mystery. The fruit is a certain virtue or grace that flows from meditation on that mystery, since it is lived in some way by Jesus or Mary in that particular event.

Focusing on a certain fruit can help us to desire it and open our hearts to it. In this booklet, there is a suggested fruit for each decade: for example, gratitude, confidence in Jesus, or increase of hope.

Intercessory Prayer: The Rosary is a very powerful form of intercessory prayer, which is prayer to God on behalf of others. While praying the Rosary, you can choose to pray for particular people, needs, or situations (prayer intentions). The words and mysteries may both fade into the background as you focus on asking Mary to lift up to God a particular person or situation that you have at heart. In this booklet, you will see one prayer intention provided for each mystery, but these, of course, are simply suggestions. You can choose to devote an entire Rosary to one intention, or each decade to a different intention, or you can pray each Hail Mary for different intentions.

Different methods and approaches to praying the Rosary work for different people or for the same person at various stages of life—or even for the same person during the praying of a single Rosary! Let the Holy Spirit lead you into new, different, or deeper forms of prayer.

How to Pray the Rosary

Begin by making the Sign of the Cross; then, while holding the crucifix of your rosary, pray the Apostles' Creed (p. 6). On the beads of the small chain, pray one Our Father (p. 6), three Hail Marys (p. 7), and one Glory (p. 7). Next, read the mystery and pray one Our Father, ten Hail Marys, and a Glory. This completes one decade. The Fatima Prayer (p. 7) and the short prayer at the end of each mystery are optional additions to conclude each decade. All of the other decades are prayed in the same manner, while meditating on the mystery for each decade. At the end, pray the Hail, Holy Queen (p. 56) and/or the Memorare (p. 56), and, if you wish, the Litany of Loreto (p. 57).

Although you can pray any of the mysteries of the Rosary on any day, they are traditionally prayed on certain days of the week:

Joyful	Monday and Saturday
Luminous	Thursday
Sorrowful	Tuesday and Friday
Glorious	Wednesday and Sunday

Rosary beads provide a physical way to keep track of the prayers so that one's mind is free to meditate on the mysteries. The diagram that follows shows how to pray the Rosary, step by step.

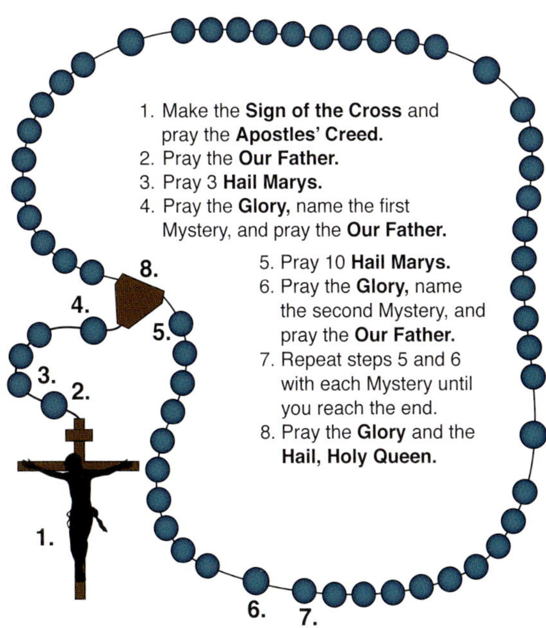

The Prayers of the Rosary

The Apostles' Creed

I believe in God, the Father almighty, creator of heaven and earth.

I believe in Jesus Christ, his only Son, our Lord.

He was conceived by the Holy Spirit and born of the Virgin Mary. He suffered under Pontius Pilate, was crucified, died and was buried. He descended into hell. On the third day he rose again. He ascended into heaven, and is seated at the right hand of the Father. He will come again to judge the living and the dead.

I believe in the Holy Spirit, the holy catholic Church, the communion of saints, the forgiveness of sins, the resurrection of the body, and the life everlasting. Amen.

The Lord's Prayer

Our Father, who art in heaven, hallowed be thy name; thy kingdom come; thy will be done on earth as it is in heaven. Give us this day our daily bread, and forgive us our trespasses, as we forgive those who trespass against us, and lead us not into temptation, but deliver us from evil. Amen.

Hail Mary

Hail Mary, full of grace! The Lord is with you. Blessed are you among women, and blessed is the fruit of your womb, Jesus. Holy Mary, Mother of God, pray for us sinners, now and at the hour of our death. Amen.

Glory

Glory be to the Father and to the Son and to the Holy Spirit. As it was in the beginning is now, and ever shall be, world without end. Amen.

Fatima Prayer

(Often prayed at the end of each decade of the Rosary.)

O my Jesus, forgive us our sins. Save us from the fires of hell; lead all souls to heaven, especially those most in need of your mercy. Amen.

The prayers that can be used at the end of the Rosary can be found on pp. 56–60.

JOYFUL MYSTERIES

First Joyful Mystery

The Annunciation

> The angel said to her, "Do not be afraid, Mary, for you have found favor with God. And now, you will conceive in your womb and bear a son, and you will name him Jesus." (Lk 1:30–31)

The first word the Angel Gabriel says to Mary is "Hail," which literally means "Rejoice!" (Lk 1:28, NABRE). The great moment had arrived. Sent by the Father, the Son of God was about to become incarnate, to become one of us, to save us from our sins. Mary joyfully consented to this invitation from God through the angel. "Here am I, the servant of the Lord" (Lk 1:38). The Holy Spirit overshadowed Mary and the Incarnation took place.

Fruit of the Mystery: Courage and trust in God
Intention: For those who are fearful and suffer from anxiety.

Holy Mary, you trusted God even though the path before you was not fully clear. Pray for me that I also may trust God in the difficulties of life and face the future with serene trust.

Second Joyful Mystery

The Visitation

> Mary set out and went with haste to a Judean town in the hill country, where she entered the house of Zechariah and greeted Elizabeth. (Lk 1:39–40)

Filled with the Holy Spirit, Mary joyfully hurried to help Elizabeth in her need. Elizabeth also received the Holy Spirit, and when Mary greeted her, Elizabeth felt the infant in her womb leap for joy. John the Baptist leapt for joy because Mary was carrying Jesus, the Son of God and her son. We also carry Jesus within us through the grace of our Baptism and can radiate his love and joy to others.

Fruit of the Mystery: Charity toward one's neighbor

Intention: For expectant mothers, especially those tempted to abort.

Mary, you brought joy to those whom you met because you were carrying Jesus within you. Pray for me that I also may communicate joy to others, because the Holy Spirit dwells in me through grace.

Third Joyful Mystery
The Birth of Jesus

She gave birth to her firstborn son and wrapped him in bands of cloth, and laid him in a manger, because there was no place for them in the inn. (Lk 2:7)

Jesus is born—the incarnate Son of God, our Savior. Mary and Joseph looked at him in wonder and love. We often forget about Joseph. Strong and silent, he watched over and protected both Mary and Jesus. He brought them to safety in Egypt when they fled from Herod. Joseph can watch over and protect us too. Saint Teresa of Ávila once said that she never asked Saint Joseph for anything without receiving it. He still intercedes for our needs.

Fruit of the Mystery: Generosity

Intention: For those who are able, that they will share with people in need.

Saint Joseph, thank you for all you did for Jesus and Mary. I want you to be part of my family too. Come to our aid in all of our needs!

Fourth Joyful Mystery

The Presentation

> When the time came for their purification according to the law of Moses, they brought him up to Jerusalem to present him to the Lord. (Lk 2:22)

Mary and Joseph brought the infant Jesus to the Temple to consecrate him to the Lord. Their joy was mixed with sorrow when Simeon prophesied that a sword would pierce Mary's heart. She pondered these mysterious words and entrusted herself to the Lord with faith. In this mystery, we remember that through Baptism we too have been consecrated to the Lord. Those in the consecrated life also commit themselves to God and the Church in a special way through their vows.

Fruit of the Mystery: Gratitude

Intention: For vocations to consecrated life.

Mary and Joseph, you were awestruck when Simeon said that Jesus would be a "light for revelation to the Gentiles" (Lk 2:32). Pray for me that by virtue of my Baptism I may bring this light to others.

Fifth Joyful Mystery

The Finding of Jesus in the Temple

> He said to them, "Why were you searching for me? Did you not know that I must be in my Father's house?" (Lk 2:49)

The Holy Family went to Jerusalem to celebrate the Passover. When Mary and Joseph realized the 12-year-old Jesus was lost, they rushed to find him. Joy flooded their hearts when they found him, but his mysterious words baffled them. Like Mary and Joseph, we can always find Jesus in his Father's house. The only thing that can separate us from Jesus is sin. But if we sin, he is always waiting for us to return to him, and he welcomes us with his mercy.

Fruit of the Mystery: Joy on life's journey
Intention: For families who are struggling to love and support one another.

Lord Jesus, I love you and want to give you my whole heart. Strengthen me that I may never turn away from you by sin. If I fall, give me confidence in your merciful love.

LUMINOUS MYSTERIES

First Luminous Mystery

The Baptism of Jesus

> "I baptize you with water for repentance, but one who is more powerful than I is coming after me. . . . He will baptize you with the Holy Spirit and fire." (Mt 3:11)

When Jesus was baptized, the heavens were opened, the Holy Spirit descended on Jesus, and the Father said, "This is my beloved Son" (Mt 3:17, NABRE). When we receive the sacrament of Baptism, we become beloved children of God by grace. Baptism forgives our sins and opens for us the path to heaven. We receive the Holy Spirit at our Baptism, who dwells in our souls, giving us the power to believe, hope, and love.

Fruit of the Mystery: A single-hearted following of Christ

Intention: For those preparing for Baptism, especially those in your parish and diocese.

Thank you, Jesus, for the gift of Baptism and the grace I have received through it. Grant me an increase of faith, hope, and love, so that I may always be faithful to that gift.

Second Luminous Mystery

Jesus Reveals His Glory at the Wedding at Cana

When the wine gave out, the mother of Jesus said to him, "They have no wine." (Jn 2:3)

Jesus had been invited to a wedding at Cana. When the wine ran out at the celebration, Mary presented the situation to him: "They have no wine." Jesus worked a miracle, the first of his "signs" in John's Gospel. Seeing this, "his disciples believed in him" (Jn 2:11). In this mystery, we can contemplate the importance of the sacrament of Marriage, and we give thanks that Mary helps us as she helped the newlyweds at Cana.

Fruit of the Mystery: Confidence in Jesus
Intention: For all engaged and married couples, especially those in particular need.

Jesus, I thank you for the gift of the sacraments, especially that of Marriage. Lord, increase my faith so that I may always firmly believe in you.

THIRD LUMINOUS MYSTERY

Jesus Preaches the Kingdom and Calls Us to Conversion

> Jesus came to Galilee . . . saying, "The time is fulfilled, and the kingdom of God has come near; repent, and believe in the good news." (Mk 1:14–15)

Jesus calls us to conversion out of love, and he does not condemn us. Jesus knows our struggles, our problems, and the weaknesses that lead us to sin. When he calls us to conversion, he also gives us the grace to overcome sin. The more we trust in Jesus, the more he can do for us. His mercy has no limits. The kingdom of God means that in Jesus, God has come near his people to rule in love.

Fruit of the Mystery: Conversion in an area of your life where you most need it

Intention: For all missionaries, at home and in other countries.

Jesus, you know the inmost thoughts of my heart. I bring to you all that needs healing within me, and I trust in your mercy and love. Help me to do better.

Fourth Luminous Mystery

The Transfiguration

And [Jesus] was transfigured before them, and his face shone like the sun, and his clothes became dazzling white. (Mt 17:2)

Jesus went up a mountain with three apostles: Peter, James, and John, and he was radiantly changed as the glory of God shone through him. The Father said: "This is my son . . . listen to him!" (Mt 17:5). What Jesus is by nature—the Son of God—we become through adoption by grace: sons and daughters of God. The more we listen to the words of Jesus, and let them enlighten us, the more we will grow in his image.

Fruit of the Mystery: Openness to the transforming light of Christ

Intention: For those who are making a retreat.

Jesus, you have the words of eternal life (see Jn 6:68). Help me to meditate on your words so that my life may reflect your love to everyone I meet.

Fifth Luminous Mystery

Jesus Gives Us the Eucharist

[Jesus] said to them, "I have eagerly desired to eat this Passover with you before I suffer." (Lk 22:15)

At the Last Supper Jesus gave us the sacrament of the Holy Eucharist: "This is my body, which is given for you. Do this in remembrance of me" (Lk 22:19). In the Eucharist, Jesus is truly present in his Body, Blood, soul, and divinity. When we receive Communion worthily, we grow in sanctifying grace, which means he lives in us and we live in him, and we can bear fruit in our lives through growth in virtue. Let us ask Jesus for a profound faith and a deep love for him in this wonderful sacrament.

Fruit of the Mystery: A deeper love and appreciation of the Eucharist

Intention: For all priests, especially those in particular difficulty.

Jesus, I thank you for the gift of yourself in the Eucharist. Help me to treasure this gift and, through it, to grow in love for you and for my neighbor.

SORROWFUL MYSTERIES

First Sorrowful Mystery

The Agony in the Garden

> [Jesus] said, "Abba, Father, for you all things are possible; remove this cup from me; yet, not what I want, but what you want." (Mk 14:36)

All his life Jesus was intent on his mission of redemption, and now the moment of his Passion and death had arrived. Though he wanted to fulfill it, he still felt the struggle and prayed to his Father for strength. Despite his agony, he fully and freely offered his life to save us from sin. Whatever trials we face, Jesus understands and is near us, because in every way he "has been tested as we are, yet without sin" (Heb 4:15).

Fruit of the Mystery: Joyful obedience to God's will

Intention: For those who are struggling to do what they know is right.

Jesus, I trust in you. Be with me through all the trials of my life and give me the strength to follow in your footsteps.

Second Sorrowful Mystery
The Scourging at the Pillar

Then Pilate took Jesus and had him flogged. (Jn 19:1)

Roman scourgings were brutal. The number of scourges was unlimited, unlike Jewish law that specified no more than forty lashes. The scourge had pieces of bone or metal attached at various intervals—designed to inflict maximum pain. Jesus suffered excruciating physical pain, and he did it out of love for us. Contemplating him like this, we ponder the words of Saint Paul: Jesus "loved me and gave himself for me" (Gal 2:20). How can I respond to such love?

Fruit of the Mystery: Forgiveness
Intention: For those struggling with resentment and bitterness.

Jesus, I love you and thank you for all you suffered in your Passion. Help me, out of love for you, to be patient in the small trials of daily life.

Third Sorrowful Mystery

The Crowning with Thorns

> After twisting some thorns into a crown, [the soldiers] put it on his head. . . . [They] knelt before him and mocked him saying, "Hail, King of the Jews!" (Mt 27:29)

The soldiers spit on Jesus, slapped and mocked him, and crowned him with sharp thorns. Jesus is a King, but not the kind of king they had in mind. As he told Pilate, "My kingdom is not from this world" (Jn 18:36). Jesus the King gave his life for us, offering it up as a sacrifice for the salvation of the world. How can I respond to his love?

Fruit of the Mystery: Humility

Intention: For those in authority, that they will work for justice for all, especially for those most in need.

I praise and thank you, Jesus, King of kings, for giving your life for me. In the sorrows of life, help me to look to you for strength.

Fourth Sorrowful Mystery

The Carrying of the Cross

> So they took Jesus; and carrying the cross by himself, he went out to what is called The Place of the Skull, which in Hebrew is called Golgotha. (Jn 19:16–17)

Jesus, already very weak from the loss of a lot of blood, was forced to carry his heavy Cross up the hill to Calvary. Fearing Jesus would die before the crucifixion, the soldiers compelled Simon of Cyrene to help him. Today we can still help Jesus by reaching out to those around us who are suffering, as he said, "Just as you did it to one of the least of these . . . you did it to me" (Mt 25:40).

Fruit of the Mystery: Patience in suffering
Intention: For those who suffer from physical, mental, or spiritual illness.

Jesus, I know you are with me as I carry my cross. Help me to be aware of others and to do what I can to help them in their suffering.

IESVS NAZARÆNVS REX IVDÆORVM

Fifth Sorrowful Mystery

The Crucifixion and Death of Jesus

> Then [the criminal crucified with him] said, "Jesus, remember me when you come into your kingdom." He replied, "Truly I tell you, today you will be with me in Paradise." (Lk 23:42–43)

After Jesus died on the cross, a soldier pierced his heart, and blood and water flowed out (see Jn 19:34). That blood and water represents the stream of divine mercy, the cleansing waters of Baptism, Penance, and the Eucharist. When we repent and draw near to Jesus, he washes us clean from all our sins. No one should approach Jesus in fear, for he said, "I will not reject anyone who comes to me" (Jn 6:37, NABRE).

Fruit of the Mystery: The grace of a good death
Intention: For those who will die today, especially those most in need of God's mercy.

Jesus, I thank you for your love for me and for inviting everyone to be with you in heaven. Help me to avoid sin and to follow you faithfully.

GLORIOUS MYSTERIES

First Glorious Mystery

The Resurrection

But the angel said to the women, "Do not be afraid; I know that you are looking for Jesus who was crucified. He is not here; for he has been raised, as he said." (Mt 28:5–6)

By rising from the dead, Jesus conquered death and brought us new life. In Baptism we are joined to Christ's death. Through him we rise to new life in God. Faith unlocks for us the great mystery of the Lord's resurrection. Jesus transforms us so that we can live a new life in union with him. Saint Paul says, "So you also must consider yourselves dead to sin and alive to God in Christ Jesus" (Rom 6:11).

Fruit of the Mystery: Growth in faith

Intention: For atheists and agnostics.

Jesus, thank you for dying and rising so that we might live in you. Help me to live in the power of the resurrection so that I may reflect your love to all I meet.

Second Glorious Mystery

The Ascension

> While [Jesus] was blessing them, he withdrew from them and was carried up into heaven. And they worshiped him, and returned to Jerusalem with great joy. (Lk 24:51–52)

As Jesus ascended into heaven, he promised, "I am with you always" (Mt 28:20). Having completed his mission from the Father, Jesus entrusted his Church with the mission to preach the Good News all over the world. As his disciples, we will face difficulties, but Jesus will always be with us, to sustain us. The virtue of hope keeps this promise alive in our hearts.

Fruit of the Mystery: An increase of hope
Intention: For those tempted to despair and suicide.

Jesus, I want to be your disciple and to share with others the great joy of the Gospel. Help me to remember I am not alone, for you are always with me.

Third Glorious Mystery
The Descent of the Holy Spirit

> When the day of Pentecost had come, they were all together in one place. And suddenly from heaven there came a sound like the rush of a violent wind. (Acts 2:1–2)

The Holy Spirit transformed the apostles in the Upper Room at Pentecost, filling them with boldness and courage. In Baptism and Confirmation we too receive the Holy Spirit, who dwells in our souls through grace. The Spirit gives us the strength we need to follow Jesus and to bring him to others. We can do this by the witness of our life and by offering encouragement to others. Just as Mary prayed with the apostles in the Upper Room, she will intercede for us too.

Fruit of the Mystery: Zeal to proclaim the Gospel
Intention: For those who use the media to evangelize.

Holy Spirit, pour into my heart the abundance of your gifts: wisdom, understanding, counsel, fortitude, knowledge, piety, and holy fear of the Lord. Be with me in each moment.

Fourth Glorious Mystery

The Assumption of Mary

From now on all generations will call me
blessed;
for the Mighty One has done great things
for me,
and holy is his name. (Lk 1:48–49)

At the end of her life, Mary was taken up to heaven, body and soul. It was fitting that God should glorify her in this way because she gave birth to the Son of God. This mystery shows us the dignity of the human body, which, by the gift of grace, becomes a temple of the Holy Spirit and is destined for glory. Mary is the woman "clothed with the sun" (Rev 12:1), our advocate and intercessor.

Fruit of the Mystery: Desire for heaven

Intention: For the souls in purgatory.

Intercede for me, Mary, our loving Mother, so that on the last day my body may be raised and reunited with my soul to live forever in heaven with you and Jesus, your risen Son.

Fifth Glorious Mystery

The Crowning of Mary Queen of Heaven and Earth

A great portent appeared in heaven: a woman clothed with the sun, with the moon under her feet, and on her head a crown of twelve stars. (Rev 12:1)

This mystery is linked with Mary's Assumption and highlights her spiritual motherhood in the Church. Her queenship is one of love and service, exercised in hearts. It reminds us that "if we endure, we will also reign with him" (2 Tm 2:12) as members of Christ's "royal priesthood" (1 Pt 2:9). As our queen in glory, Mary prays for us and walks by our side to support us in the troubles of life.

Fruit of the Mystery: Fortitude and perseverance

Intention: For those persecuted for their faith.

Mary, my Queen and Mother, I look forward to being with you and Jesus in our heavenly home. Pray for me now that I may live as a faithful disciple of Jesus.

Concluding Prayers

After the last mystery, it is common to end the Rosary with the Hail, Holy Queen or another prayer of your choice.

Hail, Holy Queen

Hail, holy Queen, Mother of mercy, our life, our sweetness, and our hope! To you we cry, poor banished children of Eve; to you we send up our sighs, mourning, and weeping in this valley of tears. Turn then, most gracious advocate, your eyes of mercy toward us, and after this our exile, show unto us the blessed fruit of your womb, Jesus. O clement, O loving, O sweet Virgin Mary.

Memorare

Remember, O most gracious Virgin Mary, that never was it known that anyone who fled to your protection, implored your help, or sought your intercession was left unaided. Inspired with this confidence, I fly to you, O Virgin of virgins, my Mother. To you I come, before you I stand, sinful and sorrowful. O Mother of the Word Incarnate, despise not my petitions, but in your mercy hear and answer me. Amen.

Litany of Loreto

Lord, have mercy on us.
Christ, have mercy on us.
Lord, have mercy on us.
Christ, hear us.
Christ, graciously hear us.
God the Father of heaven, have mercy on us.
God the Son, Redeemer of the world, have mercy on us.
God the Holy Spirit, have mercy on us.
Holy Trinity, one God, have mercy on us.
Holy Mary, *pray for us.*
Holy Mother of God, *pray for us.*
Holy Virgin of virgins, *pray for us.*
Mother of Christ, *pray for us.*
Mother of Divine Grace, *pray for us.*
Mother most pure, *pray for us.*
Mother most chaste, *pray for us.*
Mother inviolate, *pray for us.*
Mother undefiled, *pray for us.*
Mother most amiable, *pray for us.*
Mother most admirable, *pray for us.*

Mother of good counsel, *pray for us.*
Mother of our Creator, *pray for us.*
Mother of our Savior, *pray for us.*
Mother of the Church, *pray for us.*
Virgin most prudent, *pray for us.*
Virgin most venerable, *pray for us.*
Virgin most renowned, *pray for us.*
Virgin most powerful, *pray for us.*
Virgin most merciful, *pray for us.*
Virgin most faithful, *pray for us.*
Mirror of justice, *pray for us.*
Seat of wisdom, *pray for us.*
Cause of our joy, *pray for us.*
Spiritual vessel, *pray for us.*
Vessel of honor, *pray for us.*
Singular vessel of devotion, *pray for us.*
Mystical rose, *pray for us.*
Tower of David, *pray for us.*
Tower of ivory, *pray for us.*
House of gold, *pray for us.*
Ark of the covenant, *pray for us.*
Gate of Heaven, *pray for us.*
Morning star, *pray for us.*
Health of the sick, *pray for us.*
Refuge of sinners, *pray for us.*

Comforter of the afflicted, *pray for us.*
Help of Christians, *pray for us.*
Queen of angels, *pray for us.*
Queen of patriarchs, *pray for us.*
Queen of prophets, *pray for us.*
Queen of apostles, *pray for us.*
Queen of martyrs, *pray for us.*
Queen of confessors, *pray for us.*
Queen of virgins, *pray for us.*
Queen of all saints, *pray for us.*
Queen conceived without original sin, *pray for us.*
Queen assumed into Heaven, *pray for us.*
Queen of the holy Rosary, *pray for us.*
Queen of families, *pray for us.*
Queen of peace, *pray for us.*

Lamb of God, who takes away the sins of the world, spare us, O Lord.
Lamb of God, who takes away the sins of the world, graciously spare us, O Lord.
Lamb of God, who takes away the sins of the world, have mercy on us.

℣. Pray for us, O holy Mother of God,
℟. that we may be made worthy of the promises of Christ.

Let us pray.

O God, whose only-begotten Son, by his life, death, and resurrection, has purchased for us the rewards of eternal life, grant, we beseech you, that by meditating upon these mysteries of the most holy Rosary of the Blessed Virgin Mary, we may imitate what they contain, and obtain what they promise. Through Christ our Lord. Amen.

℣. May the divine assistance always remain with us.

℟. And may the souls of the faithful departed, through the mercy of God, rest in peace. Amen.

Indulgences

When the Rosary is prayed in a group, as in a church after daily Mass, at the very end you may hear the leader add an extra Our Father, Hail Mary, and Glory "for the intentions of the Holy Father." The reason for this is that prayer for the intentions of the pope is one of the requirements for gaining a plenary indulgence, which is available for praying the Rosary.

Briefly, an indulgence is the remission of temporal punishment due to sin. When we repent from sin and turn back to God, he forgives us and removes all eternal punishment for our sin. But there is still a wound, or a sinful attachment that remains and needs to be purified. This is why we say that there is temporal punishment due to sin. Indulgences remove temporal punishment either in part (partial) or in whole (plenary). As the *Catechism of the Catholic Church* teaches, "Every sin, even venial, entails an unhealthy attachment to creatures, which must be purified either here on earth, or after death in the state called Purgatory" (no. 1472).

A plenary indulgence can be received when the Rosary is recited in a church, a family, a religious community, or a pious association. A partial indulgence is granted for its recitation in all other circumstances.

Indulgences can be for oneself or they can be applied to the dead who are in purgatory. To gain a plenary indulgence for praying the Rosary while meditating on the mysteries, one must also go to confession* and receive Communion (within 20 days before or after), pray for the intentions of the pope, and be detached from all sin.

* While all the other conditions must be fulfilled for each plenary indulgence, one confession can suffice for several. So to gain a daily plenary indulgence one must go to confession at least once every 20 days and receive Communion daily.